My Very First Look at
Sizes

LONDON · PRINCETON

www.two-canpublishing.com

Published by Two-Can Publishing,
43–45 Dorset Street, London W1U 7NA

© 2002 Two-Can Publishing

For information on Two-Can books and multimedia,
call (0)20 7224 2440, fax (0)20 7224 7005, or visit our
website at http://www.two-canpublishing.com

Conceived, designed and edited by

Picthall & Gunzi Ltd

21A Widmore Road, Bromley, Kent BR1 1RW

Original concept: Chez Picthall
Editor: Lauren Robertson
Designer: Dominic Zwemmer
Photography: Steve Gorton
Additional photographs: Daniel Pangbourne
DTP: Tony Cutting, Ray Bryant
Cover design: Paul Calver

'Two-Can' is a trademark of Two-Can Publishing.
Two-Can Publishing is a division of Zenith Entertainment Ltd,
43–45 Dorset Street, London W1U 7NA.

HC ISBN 1–85434–940–6
SC ISBN 1-84301-044-5

HC 2 3 4 5 6 7 8 9 10 04 03 02
SC 1 2 3 4 5 6 7 8 9 10 04 03 02

A catalogue record for this book is available from the British Library.

Colour reproduction by Next Century Ltd.
Printed in Italy.

My Very First Look at
Sizes

Christiane Gunzi

LONDON · PRINCETON

Big and small

shells

balls

Can you see something square?

Can you point to the pink one?

Big, bigger, biggest

Which ball has the most colours?

What colour is the biggest ball?

Small, smaller, smallest

How many blue beads are there?

What colour is the biggest bead?

Long and short

bread

hair ribbons

Which of these can you eat?

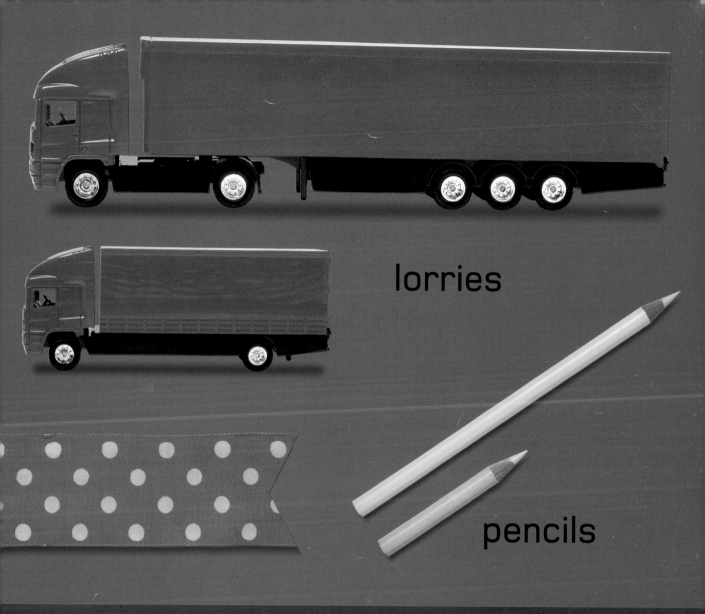

lorries

pencils

What colours are the ribbons?

Thick and thin

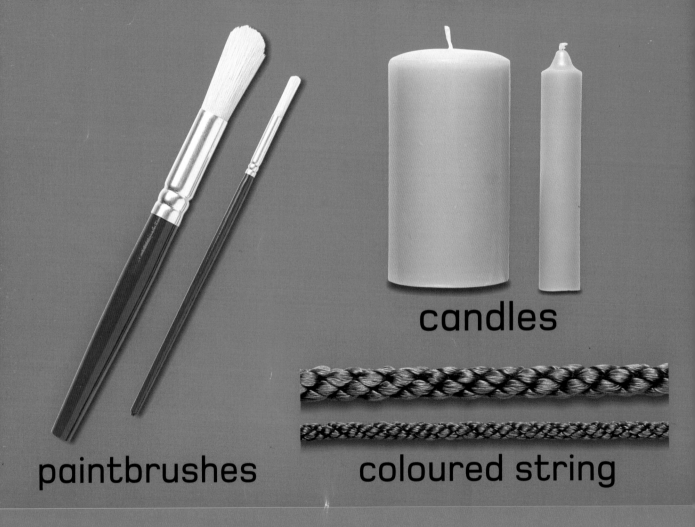

candles

paintbrushes

coloured string

What colour are the candles?

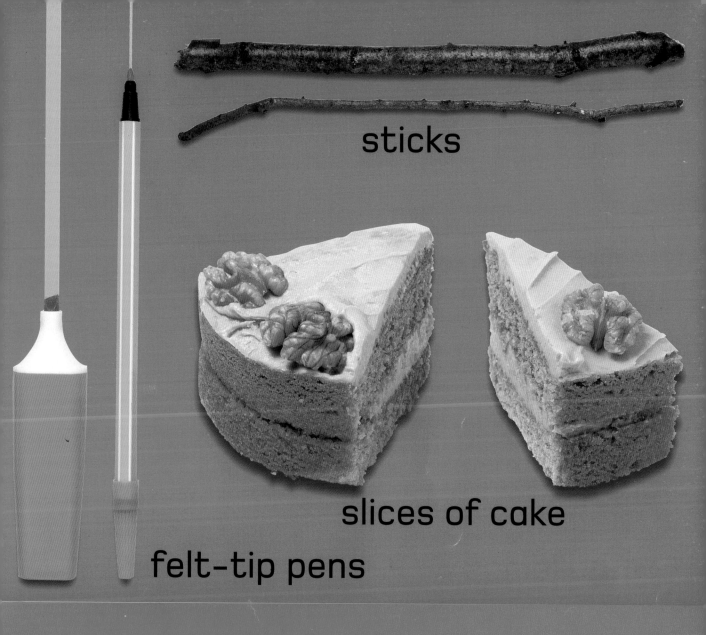

sticks

slices of cake

felt-tip pens

Can you write with any of these?

Tall and short

buildings

giraffes

How many windows can you see?

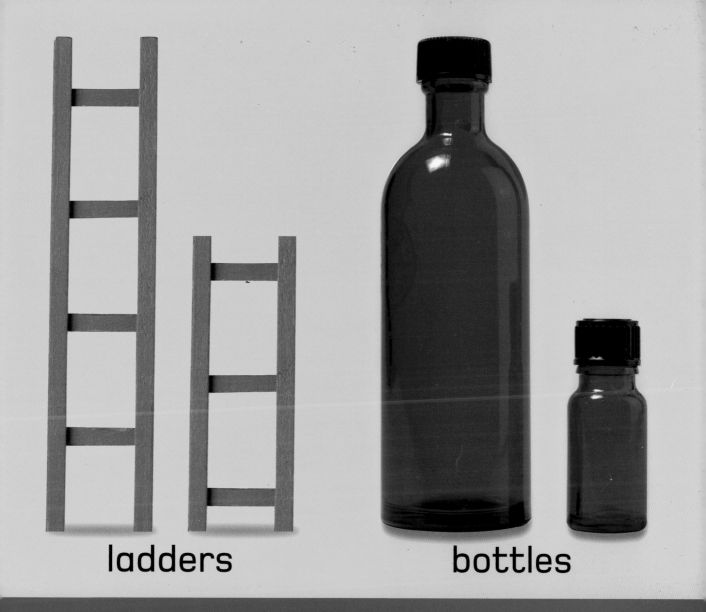

ladders

bottles

Can you point to the tall ladder?

Same size

shell

stone

sticky tape

flower

cake

apple

Which of these is orange?

eggs

gloves

shoes

balls

How many balls can you see?

Different sizes

car

tile

beads

mug

bar of chocolate

Which thing is the biggest?

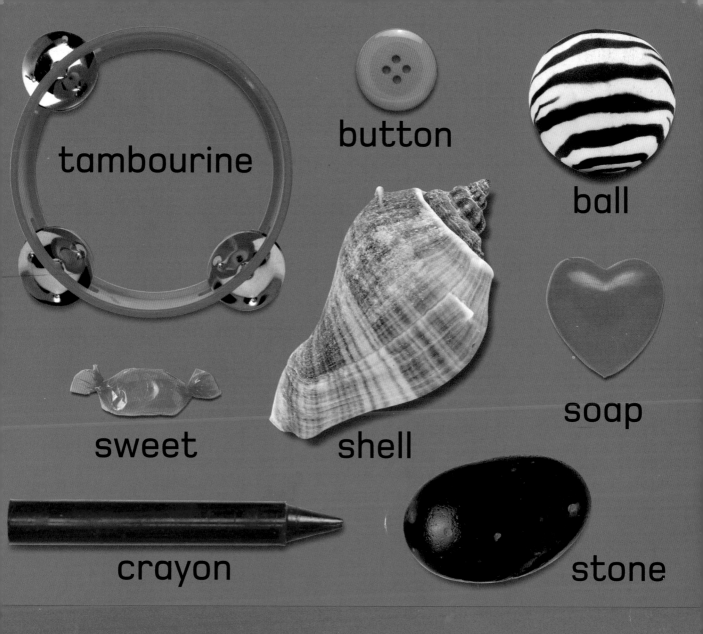

tambourine

button

ball

shell

soap

sweet

crayon

stone

Which thing is the smallest?

What size?

balls

giraffes

bread

Which of these is the tallest?